THE JOY OF | Cockatiels

HOWARD RICHMOND

Photography: Eliot Goldfinger, title page, 16 (top), 32 (top), 37, 41, 44 (bottom), 52, 57, 64, 73 (bottom), 80 (top), 84-85, 89 (top), 93. Nancy Richmond, 4, 8, 9, 12, 13, 16 (bottom), 17, 20, 21, 24-25, 28, 32 (bottom), 33, 36, 40, 44 (top), 45, 48, 49, 56, 60-61, 65, 68, 72, 73 (top), 76, 77, 80 (bottom), 81, 88, 89 (bottom), 92. Vincent Serbin, 23, 47 (top).

ISBN 0-87666-554-7

Distributed in the UNITED STATES by T.F.H. Publications, Inc., 211 West Sylvania Avenue, Neptune City, NJ 07753; in CANADA by H & L Pet Supplies Inc., 27 Kingston Crescent, Kitchener, Ontario N2B 2T6; Rolf C. Hagen Ltd., 3225 Sartelon Street, Montreal 382 Quebec; in ENGLAND by T.F.H. Publications Limited, 4 Kier Park, Ascot, Berkshire SL5 7DS; in AUSTRALIA AND THE SOUTH PACIFIC by T.F.H. (Australia) Pty. Ltd., Box 149, Brookvale 2100 N.S.W., Australia; in NEW ZEALAND by Ross Haines & Son, Ltd., 18 Monmouth Street, Grey Lynn, Auckland 2 New Zealand; in SINGAPORE AND MALAYSIA by MPH Distributors Pte., 71-77 Stamford Road, Singapore 0617; in the PHILIPPINES by Bio-Research, 5 Lippay Street, San Lorenzo Village, Makati, Rizal; in SOUTH AFRICA by Multipet Pty. Ltd., 30 Turners Avenue, Durban 4001. Published by T.F.H. Publications Inc., Ltd., the British Crown Colony of Hong Kong.

Contents

This responsible young boy acquired his pet cockatiel when it was still a juvenile, ten to twelve weeks old. Young cockatiels make better pets because they are more receptive to taming and training. In time, after several training sessions, the bird will learn that its owner's shoulder is a secure place on which to perch.

Cockatiels as Pets

If you walk into any pet shop that sells birds, you are sure to find many birds that are members of the parrot order. Some of these brightly colored creatures are well-known for their ability to imitate the human voice, some for their brilliant plumage, while others seem to have affectionate personalities. Of the many pet birds usually available in pet shops, cockatiels seem to be ideal pets: highly personable, exhibiting amusing antics, easy to care for, and having a talent for mimicry. This graceful, distinctively colored parrot, known to science as *Nymphicus hollandicus*, is often called a "quarrion" in Australia. Second only to budgerigars in popularity, cockatiels may be purchased at a relatively low cost, are easy to tame and train, and excel as household pets. Cockatiels continue to gain wide acceptance among owners of pet birds.

Ancient history tells of many instances in which parrots were kept as pets. They had been brought from India to ancient Greece. Romans too brought parrots back to their native land from Africa. Later, European explorers, venturing into tropical countries new to them, found native Indians keeping tamed parrots as household pets. Still, although parrots had been kept as pets for many hundreds of years, it was only with the introduction of Australian species, including cockatiels and budgerigars, that parrots attracted wide attention. The popularity of cockatiels and budgerigars soon spread throughout the world.

One of the most readily distinguished groups of parrots, because of anatomy, is the cockatoos. All are native to the

Pacific region. They stand out because of their movable crests and subtle coloration. They never have the bright colors many other parrots do. Many believe that the smallest of the cockatoos is the cockatiel. The crest bears this out, but there is a considerable difference in appearance between the long-tailed cockatiel and the larger, more stockily built, short-tailed cockatoos.

The Wild Cockatiel

The cockatiel is indigenous to Australia. In their native habitat, they travel and nest in flocks, often in the same areas as budgerigars. The cockatiel leads a nomadic existence. Ranging through openly forested areas and savannas in the arid central regions of the continent, cockatiels feed on the seeds of a number of grasses, varied herbage such as leaves and bark, as well as fruits and berries. The availability of water to a great extent determines their wanderings; often they must cover vast areas in order to survive. Being nomadic, they may appear almost anywhere throughout the interior of Australia, but they usually avoid the coastal areas except in periods of extreme drought.

In the wild they may breed oftener than once a year, the frequency being dependent upon the food supply. It is not unusual for a large flock of cockatiels to remain for some time in an area offering favorable living conditions, perhaps rearing several broods in succession. When the growing number of young birds or the changing seasons begins to limit the available food supply, most of the birds move on.

The rapid growth of vegetation resulting from the rainy season usually triggers the start of breeding. Cockatiels nest in hollows in the trunks of trees. Should the cavity be too small, the birds use their beaks to scoop out the soft parts of the tree. Most often they choose a nest location that affords them a good view in all directions.

Like budgerigars, they are opportunistic breeders and are inclined to breed in captivity whenever the conditions are right. As a result cockatiels have become widely available as pets. To satisfy the demand for pet birds many large commercial breeding operations have come into being. Because of the growth of commercial breeding, as well as the prohibition on exporting birds from Australia, no cockatiel that you encounter will be wild caught. All will have been bred in captivity.

Cockatiels as Companions

It is because cockatiels are well adapted to the vicissitudes of a relatively harsh environment that they are successful as cage birds. They are accustomed to a diet that is simple—compared to that demanded by many bird species—and the components of this diet are items that those who keep the birds can easily supply. In addition to being hardy by nature and easy to feed, cockatiels are clean birds requiring only minimum care.

One of the characteristics that adds a great deal to the attraction of pet cockatiels is that they enjoy being stroked about the head. They do not seem to mind being handled as much as some other bird species, and may even enjoy being picked up. This derives from their natural behavior: normally living in small flocks in the wild, the cockatiel is essentially a social bird. They are so gregarious that when the flock settles on a dead tree, most birds perch together on the same branch. This sociable behavior evident in the wild becomes in captivity an attachment to the bird keeper.

Like other parrots, cockatiels are very capable climbers because of the structure of their feet. Also, they use their hooked bill as a third foot, to pull themselves forward among branches or along tree trunks. This tendency to use the bill as a means of locomotion, combined with climbing activities and their inclination toward preening, results in a number of highly amusing antics, often endearing the bird to its owner. Here again natural behaviors are the foundation for the appeal birds like cockatiels have as pets.

Pieds (*above*) and Lutinos (*facing page*) are two of the commonly available color varieties of cockatiels.

Cockatiels are one of many species of parrots that can be taught to imitate human words with amazing fidelity. There is no evidence that parrots ever use their remarkable powers of imitation in the wild, but in captivity, when kept in close contact with human beings but away from their own kind, many individuals will mimic their human keepers. They soon learn that the vocalization of words they often hear results in an increase in the amount of attention they receive from their human companions. It's likely that the learning of human speech by pet birds stems from their need for social relationship.

For some people, a parrot alone in its cage is a sad sight. It needs a companion, they feel. But if a single cockatiel has adequate human companionship, it will not be lonely. This means that if you are planning to keep a single cockatiel, you must give it the attention it needs. The happiest single birds are those that do become tame and interact with their owners. Untamed birds usually are neglected eventually, with unfortunate results. If you find that you are unable to tame your cockatiel, or that you no longer have the time to keep it company, then obtaining a second cockatiel can be the solution. Two cockatiels kept together will be much more interested in one another than they are in you. This is particularly true if they are male and female, for cockatiels are inclined to form strong pair bonds.

You must have your purpose clear in mind before you go shopping for a cockatiel. If you desire a cockatiel that will be an affectionate pet, then we recommend purchasing a single bird. This book, then, is written for the person who wants to keep a single pet cockatiel. The considerations involved in keeping pairs or colonies of cockatiels—for breeding, perhaps—are not discussed here.

Shopping for a Pet

In shopping for a pet cockatiel, you will be fortunate if you are able to choose from several sources. Outlets specializing in birds are more likely to stock outstanding individual cockatiels. While some sources may sell only livestock, others will offer one-stop shopping. Besides the cockatiel, you will need food, a cage, and various accessories. It certainly is advantageous to purchase your cockatiel from a nearby location so that the seller of the bird can be consulted for additional advice. You will want to deal with people who are able to give you satisfactory, knowledgeable answers to your questions.

It is essential that you patronize an establishment where the birds are kept under the very best of conditions. Perhaps above all else, cleanliness of the place where you plan to buy your cockatiel should be a primary consideration. As you visit the places where birds are sold, look for a clean situation, where the general appearance of the birds is one of health. Look for well-maintained cages. Food and water containers should also reflect daily care. Since clean conditions are essential to the well-being of any living creature, you will want to purchase your cockatiel from an environment that shows the birds have been carefully maintained and cared for in sanitary surroundings.

Youngsters for Taming

It is generally agreed that a bird to be kept as a pet should be acquired when it is young. Have you ever wondered why? For all birds the weeks after they leave the nest are a most important period. It is during this time that they learn to adapt to the environment in which they find themselves. It is also at this time that the birds are most receptive to taming and training. They can also be taught to sample various foods.

The tamest and most affectionate cockatiels are those that have been hand-reared. These youngsters become attached to the person taking over the role of parent, and this affection for people is transferred to other owners. It's also possible that breeders give frequent handling to cockatiel

Most of the cockatiels offered for sale will not be hand-tame like this specimen (*above*). A mature Normal cock (*facing page*). Older birds make suitable pets, although generally they are more difficult to hand-tame than younger birds.

nestlings, even though they are still being fed by their natural parents; these youngsters are also especially tame. Obtaining a tame cockatiel may be worth quite a lot to you, for it can save you time. If you should be able to find such a bird, expect to pay a bit more money for it.

You can tell if a bird is somewhat tame, as it will not become too excited when a person approaches the cage. If you wish to see if a cockatiel is hand-tamed, insert your hand into the cage very slowly, palm down. Move the side of your hand towards the bird's feet. If it calmly accepts this approach, it has probably been hand-tamed.

Most of the cockatiels you encounter will probably not be tame. You will therefore have to do the taming and training yourself. This task will be easiest if you acquire a young bird, one between ten and sixteen weeks old. Older birds can still become good pets, but it's likely to require more effort on your part.

A cockatiel younger than ten weeks of age may not be completely self-feeding yet. While it's rare that too young a bird is offered for sale, you must be certain that the bird is able to eat on its own.

There are several indicators that can give you an adequate idea of a cockatiel's age. In general, juveniles have less dense feathering than adults, so they look slimmer. Often this more sparse feathering is most obvious in the crest. But for our purposes, the beak gives the best clues: it will change from pinkish to gray in the period between eight and twelve weeks of age, approximately. The youngest suitable candidates therefore will have bills that show some gray (of course, this will not occur in those color varieties in which dark pigment is suppressed).

Around about six months of age, most cockatiels will have attained adult plumage, which is most apparent in the brightness of the cheek patches, particularly of the males. For a more exact knowledge of a cockatiel's age, you will have to rely upon the person from whom you purchase the bird. Not only is the seller in a better position to know, but he likely has also had a great deal more experience in judging age.

Many prospective pet owners are interested in how long the animal will live. There are reports of cockatiels alive at twenty-five, but this is equivalent to people living until they are a hundred. It's more realistic to think of your cockatiel living for ten to fifteen years.

Sexing Cockatiels

Determination of the sex of a juvenile cockatiel is next to impossible. This is because young males and females both have the feathering and coloration of a female until they experience their first molt. Although a number of features in a growing bird seem to be indicative of sex, none are foolproof. For this reason it is thought not to be important to discuss methods of sexing that are not always valid. Additionally, it makes little difference whether you obtain a male or a female for a family pet. They are equally lovable, and one is as fascinating as the other. Both can be tamed and trained easily, and both make equally fine pets—though some authorities feel that a male cockatiel will be superior to a female in talking ability.

After the molt which occurs when the birds are around six months old, the differences between the sexes becomes obvious, in most varieties of cockatiels at least. Cockatiels that have the coloration found in the wild are called "Normals." The basic color is dark gray, with a prominent white patch of feathers on the wings. The head is capped by a crest, and the bill, eyes, and feet of mature birds are black. The distinctive features of the male are the bright orange cheek patch and the yellow coloring on the head. The crest is a mixture of yellow and gray. The total length of the male is about 13 inches. Generally, the body color of the hen is much like that of the cock; however, the plumage is duller and less distinctive. She can easily be differentiated from

Pet shops supply not only livestock, but also informative books on the subject of cockatiel care (*above*) and all of the accessories you may need (*below*). Cockatiels are available in a variety of colors, including Normal, Lutino, Pied, and Pearl (*facing page*).

the male by the barred pattern on the undersides of the wing and tail feathers.

Color Varieties

The coloration of the Normal cockatiel is produced by two groups of pigments, called *melanins* and *carotenoids.* The melanins produce the gray color of the Normal, while the yellow is a carotenoid. The orange of the cheek patch is probably a carotenoid too. Variation in the deposit of these pigments in the feathers is responsible for the differences in appearance in mutation cockatiels. In the "Pied" and the "Pearl," melanin is absent from certain feathers, or areas of feathers, as compared to the Normal. With the "Lutino," melanin is completely absent from the feathers, so the persisting carotenoids become more visible. On the other hand, it is the carotenoids that are absent from the "White-face," so its appearance is due entirely to the presence of melanins. If both pigments were absent, the result would be a true albino cockatiel. This variety has been achieved recently, by combining the genetic factors responsible for the Lutino and the White-face.

All these color varieties have occurred in captivity. The earliest are by now well established and are frequently available. Most common are Lutinos, Pieds, and Pearls.

The Lutino, comprising individuals that range from almost white to a good yellow, is one of the most popular. As we've said, this variety is not a true albino; even to call it white is misleading. Color is still present, in the orange cheek patch, for example, and there is always at least a tinge of yellow in the plumage. Because of the lack of pigment in their eyes, Lutinos often appear to be sensitive to bright light.

When this variety first appeared, it took the avicultural world by storm because it so closely resembled a miniature white cockatoo with a pale yellow crest and an almost white body, tail, and wings.

In the cock bird, the least yellow is found in the areas that are gray in the Normal cockatiel. The throat, part of the cheeks, and the front of the head are lemon yellow. The crest is a mixture of yellow and white, and the ear-patches are the normal shade of red-orange. The wings have areas of yellow and there is a yellow cast or tinge on the tail. The eyes are red, the beak is a yellow horn color, and the legs and feet are flesh pink.

Although difficult to sex at a distance, the adult hens, however light, still show some of the yellow barring on the undersides of the tail and the wings.

The Pearl cockatiel exhibits a change of pattern on the feathers. In this variety the nape of the neck, mantle, and the upper wing coverts are the areas always affected, the feathers exhibiting a scalloped effect. The same pattern is sometimes found on the breast. The Pearl effect results from white or pale yellow feathers that are edged in gray and also contain a small gray area in the center of each feather.

While the Pearl markings are found on all young birds, the cock birds lose them after the first molt. Most Pearl males can be distinguished from Normal males during the first year because they continue to carry a few pale, flecked feathers on the back or the shoulders. Also, most males will carry a slight amount of yellow at the base of each tail feather.

Pied cockatiels show great variance in markings. Those birds having mostly clear feathers in the wings, tail, head, and chest are considered "good" Pieds. The desired symmetrical pattern, the same on both sides of the bird, is rarely seen. No two birds are exactly alike.

The Pied cock is similar in color to the Normal and has clear patches of differing sizes that interrupt the dark color. These clear, irregularly shaped patches are either white or yellow tinted with white. The beak and eyes are like those of a Normal, but the feet and legs may be gray, pink, or a

Pearl cockatiels (*above and facing page*) are characterized by a mottled pattern of yellow and white spots that are found throughout the plumage, particularly on the upper wing coverts and extending across the mantle. The pearl markings may vary from one individual bird to another.

mixture of both.

The following cockatiel varieties are not often available at present, but we can expect that one day they will be. In the "Cinnamon," the melanin pigment is brown, not black, so the birds have a tannish color. The male is a darker shade than the female. An even lighter brown shade is found in "Fallow" cockatiels. The Fallow can be conceived of as a dilute version of the Cinnamon; similarly, the "Silver" shows the gray of the Normal in a lighter, diluted form.

The most recent genetic change in cockatiels is responsible for the White-face. This variety is unique in that it does not have the orange cheek patch seen in all other cockatiel varieties. The White-face does not carry any yellow pigment; without the yellow, the melanin produces a sooty charcoal color. Although both sexes look the same before the first molt, being entirely gray on the head, afterwards the face of the male becomes white. Since the White-face lacks all yellow, it can be easily distinguished from other varieties at a very young age: it has white down. While the female retains the barring underneath the tail and wing feathers, the bars are black and white.

Finally, there is the true albino cockatiel, of which only a few individuals have so far been bred.

Selecting for Health

You may have decided by now which cockatiel variety appeals to you most, and you may be eager to hurry out and find one. Before you do, though, allow yourself sufficent time—time to read a bit more about these charming birds, time to look over a representative number of birds, and time to figure out why you are going to buy a bird in the first place. Selection of a cockatiel is best accomplished by an informed individual. The second point is often overlooked, particularly by a person purchasing his first bird. Once you have found a cockatiel of interest to you, wait! By all means indicate your interest to the salesperson who has shown you

Before purchasing your pet cockatiel, observe the signs of good health in the candidate you are considering. Look for an active bird with clear eyes, unclogged nostrils, and smooth plumage, one that obviously has been maintained in a clean environment with other healthy birds.

the bird and let him know that you will come back to see the bird again. The idea is to view the bird at least two or three times, if at all possible. In this way you are able to ensure that you will be buying an alert, healthy bird. By visiting the bird on more than one occasion, you are more likely to detect any abnormalities in its behavior or health.

Choosing a healthy bird is not always a simple matter. There are a number of indicators of good health you should be aware of. In selecting a bird, look for an alert, inquisitive appearance. The eyes of a healthy bird are bright and clear; it is sleek and tight feathered. Only a bird that gives an appearance of well-being should be a candidate for purchase. A bird that spends most of its time with its feathers fluffed up, its eyes closed or swollen, shows discharge from its nostrils, or has a soiled vent should not be considered.

The plumage should be smooth, and the bird should have

Bird playgrounds provide great entertainment for cockatiels that have been let out of their cage.

no bare spots. Broken feathers will grow back in time, so you should not be concerned about them.

Its eyes should be open most of the time and free of any discharge or swelling. Birds that constantly scratch at their eyes, hold one eye closed or have a swelling around an eye probably have an eye problem that is just beginning to develop; they should not be considered.

The nasal openings should be neither clogged nor runny, and there should be no growths on the horny areas of the beak, the cere, or elsewhere. Breathing should be quiet and steady. Labored, noisy, or irregular breathing may be an indicator of respiratory distress.

Should you see a bird you like, ask to have it removed from the cage. While the bird is being held, check its vent for stains and feel the breast to be sure it is not underweight. The breastbone should not protrude. At the same time make sure there are no sores or wounds anywhere on its body.

If you find that the cockatiel you've chosen is suitable, you should now come to a clear agreement with the seller about guarantees. While some dealers will guarantee health, allow exchanges, or refund the purchase price, others do not feel that they can do so—just as you may not be prepared to guarantee that you won't be ill a week from today. But no matter what the laws or policies are that prevail in your area, this is the time to find out about them.

Since you may not feel confident about handling your cockatiel, it is suggested that you ask the seller to do certain tasks for you. You will want your cockatiel to be free of any external parasites when you take it home; ask the seller to ensure this. If the cockatiel's claws need trimming, watch the seller to see how it's done. To facilitate taming, as you'll read later on, it is recommended that the cockatiel's wing feathers be trimmed. Again, watching an experienced person do this will give you confidence if you wish to trim the feathers again, after they are molted.

Bringing Your Pet Home

Though you've made your purchase, you should not take your cockatiel home immediately, unless you've already set up a cage and have everything ready.

It's best to bring your new cockatiel home early in the day, so it will have as much time as possible to become acquainted with its new surroundings. The bird should be carried home in a cardboard box having air holes in its sides. If the day is cool, keep it warm while it's being transported, to safeguard it against becoming chilled. It is not advisable to transport a bird in the rain, not even in a covered box, because of the possibility that it may catch cold.

What you should do first with the cockatiel when you arrive home will depend on how it has reacted to being transported. The pros and cons of beginning taming at once are taken up in a later chapter. Just be certain that you watch the bird's behavior closely from the time you take it from the transport box. In any case, apart from definite taming sessions, for the first few days the cockatiel should not be constantly disturbed. Allow it sufficient opportunity to settle into its cage and new environment.

To make the transition from place to place easier, make sure that the bird is warm enough for the first few days—the room where the cage has been placed should be as warm as the space in which the bird was housed previously. An important way to ease the transition is to bring home some of the seed mix the cockatiel has been used to eating.

A cuttlebone can easily be fastened to the cockatiel's cage. Besides providing essential minerals, especially calcium, the cuttlebone helps keep the cockatiel's beak in good condition as a result of the bird's regular gnawing and chewing habits.

Feeding
and
Housing

One of the special advantages of cockatiels as pets is the ease of feeding them. Their requirements are few and simple, making them easy to keep. Healthy cockatiels are rarely a problem to feed. Like other pet animals, they will do best if given a varied and balanced diet. To prevent problems from arising, feed only recommended foods.

Seed Mixtures

In the wild, seeds of a number of different grasses are the principal food of cockatiels. Thus the basis for the daily diet of those kept in captivity is a seed mixture prepared specifically for cockatiels. Only such seed mixtures should be used. The basic seed mixture mostly includes millets, oats, and sunflower seeds as the chief ingredients, usually.

One will find different kinds of cockatiel seed mixes on the market. In addition to the brand-name products packaged by a number of large companies, many pet shops and bird specialty stores sell "house mixtures."

For the keeper of a single bird, it is best to purchase fresh seed in small quantities, lest it become stale or spoil. An easy method of testing the freshness of seeds is to place a small amount of seed in a shallow dish after having moistened it thoroughly. If the seed mixture is fresh and you have not allowed it to dry out, more than fifty percent of the seed should sprout in a few days.

Although it may be necessary to sprinkle seed on the bottom of the cage at first, until your new cockatiel has found and begun to take food from the seed cup, placing the seed mixture in the cup only is preferred.

Most of the seed supplied to cockatiels is unhulled. You'll notice that the bird eats the kernel but discards the hull. When you check the seed cup, make sure you don't mistake the hulls that may be in there for uneaten seed. Many people unused to keeping birds have made this mistake, and the bird starved to death.

It's worthwhile to get an idea of how much seed your cockatiel usually eats each day. If you know what its normal eating habits are, you will notice immediately if it starts to eat less, perhaps because of illness. You will also be able to leave your bird alone for a long weekend, secure that you have left ample seed in the cage. (This same advice applies to water, too.)

Fruits and Vegetables

The average bird keeper may not realize the benefits of feeding fruits and vegetables. The vitamin and mineral content of these foods makes them an essential part of your bird's diet. They are necessary for maintaining prime condition, giving your cockatiel its bright eyes and sleek appearance. A cockatiel should be given a portion of fruits or vegetables daily if it is to remain in healthy condition throughout the year. The bird eats wild greens such as chickweed, shepherd's purse, plantain, dandelion, and foxtail. These foods are often not readily available, but it will enjoy many which are, such as spinach, cabbage hearts, brussels sprouts, watercress, and carrot tops. Apple and pear are usually the favorite fruits. Unripened sunflower seeds from one's own garden may be offered too; in fact, a cockatiel is particularly partial to them.

Feed only as much as the bird will eat in a few hours, then remove any leftovers. Vegetables and fruits must not be allowed to wilt and become dirty on the floor of the cage. They should be given to the bird only when fresh. It is essential that all vegetables and fruits be thoroughly washed in warm water to remove any trace of pesticides; even a small amount left on these foods can be fatal. When you first feed fruits or vegetables, your cockatiel may not seem to be interested, probably because it is not accustomed to them. If you continue to offer some each day, your bird will eventually become curious and try them. After a few nibbles, it will eat them each day.

Akin to feeding fruits and vegetables is the practice of offering soaked or sprouted seeds. While the benefits of this are most directly related to breeding pairs of cockatiels, there's no reason not to afterwards feed the seed you've sprouted to test the freshness of the mix. If you enjoy sprouted grains in your own meals, it does not take a minute to serve some up for your cockatiel.

While the diet of cockatiels in the wild consists mostly of seed, this is not only the ripe, harvested seed found in the cockatiel mix you will be buying. Wild cockatiels have access to seeds in various stages of ripeness, and other vegetable matter as well, depending on the locale and the season. The bird owner can hope only to approximate this state of affairs, particularly since the cockatiel is prevented from searching out the food it may need. In practice, though, the basic daily diet of seed mix accompanied by a variety of fruits and vegetables has proved successful.

Considering the success of the species as a whole, it's obvious that wild cockatiels are able to regulate their diet themselves; however, it's reasonable to suppose that some individuals do a better job of this than others. Thus you should be wary of trusting your pet cockatiel to eat only what it needs. It's more often the case that parrot pets eat too much of their favorite foods. It may happen, for example, that your cockatiel will want to eat sunflower seed exclusively, and become too fat.

In this connection let's consider other foods you might offer. Spray millet is usually enjoyed immensely. Tugging the seeds out of the head provides activity as well as food. This is similar to many "treats" made especially for cocka-

...From T.F.H., the world's largest publisher of bird books, a new bird magazine for birdkeepers all over the world...

CAGED BIRD HOBBYIST
IS FOR EVERYONE
WHO LOVES BIRDS.

CAGED BIRD HOBBYIST
IS PACKED WITH VALUABLE
INFORMATION SHOWING HOW
TO FEED, HOUSE, TRAIN AND CARE
FOR ALL TYPES OF BIRDS.

Subscribe right now so you don't miss a single copy! SM-316

The c
seed f
this se
seed a
to bot

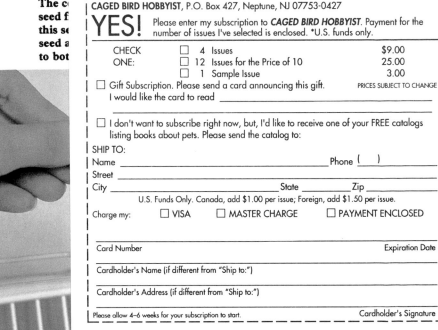
32

tiels, which are mostly seeds held together with some kind of binder. Remember, though, that treats should be used as the name implies, sparingly. Treat foods should be only a small part of a cockatiel's daily food intake. Cheese, most likely a yellow cheddar, is also relished by many cockatiels. It is a good source of calcium, which brings up another aspect of a cockatiel's diet: minerals.

Minerals

Because of the importance of calcium in the growth of feathers and bone, it is recommended that a cuttlebone always be in your cockatiel's cage. In addition, chewing on the cuttlebone provides activity and helps keep the cockatiel's beak trim. Also available are mineral blocks. The better of these are manufacturered to include small amounts of other minerals besides the primary component, calcium.

This need for minerals is recognized in another product prepared for birds, called "grit." Grit has two main ingredients: digestively insoluble particles of gravel are mixed with other particles, such as crushed oyster shell, charcoal, mineral salts, and the like, all of which yield their mineral content in the course of digestion.

At present, the practice of offering gravel (and therefore grit) to cage birds is controversial, because gravel has lately been implicated in digestive illnesses. The complicated questions involved will not soon be resolved. However, it can be said that here and there cockatiels are now living apparently healthy lives, both with access to gravel and without it. But while it's uncertain whether the insoluble particles we call gravel are beneficial to a bird's digestion, there is no question about the necessity of minerals. Your cockatiel does require these, in whatever forms they are offered: cuttlebone, mineral blocks, completely digestible grit, or powdered mineral supplements.

Besides mineral supplements, other products are designed to provide vitamins and amino acids, while still others combine all three. Oils, such as cod liver oil and wheat germ oil, are seen as sources of vitamins, primarily. It is important to remember that dietary supplements are indeed supplements. They may or may not be needed by your cockatiel, depending on a variety of factors: what is provided in the basic daily diet; the environment in which it lives and the amount of exercise it gets; and, finally, the bird's own constitution and food preferences. The considerations that figure in your cockatiel's diet are every bit as complicated as those that determine how you regulate your own diet.

As you've heard, a diet that is varied has the best chance of being nutritionally balanced. Hence it has been recommended that you offer your cockatiel a variety of foods. There is another approach to providing a balanced diet, however: the use of food pellets. Owners of dogs and cats have long been familiar with "dry foods"; the same sort of thing has lately become available for seedeating birds. The convenience of feeding your cockatiel pellets is obvious, so it may be worthwhile to undertake the task of accustoming your bird to what will most likely be unfamiliar food. Keep in mind that a diet of pellets, like any other diet, must always be monitored. It can happen that a cockatiel, like any other living organism, will need to have its diet adjusted from time to time, depending on circumstances.

One event that is often mentioned in this connection is the molt. As the annual replacement of feathers can be physically stressful for your cockatiel, it is a time to be particularly careful that the bird's diet is ample—not different, just ample.

Water

Although cockatiels do not drink a great deal of water, it is important that they always have access to a fresh supply. The water container should be kept scrupulously clean. Fresh water should be given once a day, and the water con-

Feeding a tame cockatiel by hand strengthens the bird's trust in you, and it can be a rewarding pastime for both the owner and the bird (*above*). Houseplants (*below*) are fair game for a cockatiel that has been let out of its cage.

Birds require clean, fresh water, and cockatiels are no exception to this rule. Here a pampered pet takes a sip from its keeper's glass. Normally, though, water should be offered in a container or drinking vessel that has been attached to the bird's cage.

tainer should be cleaned thoroughly each time fresh water is provided.

Besides a container for water, two or three other dishes to hold food will be necessary—which brings up the cage and its furnishings.

Cage Location

Before you decide to purchase your cockatiel and bring him home, everything necessary for the bird's comfort and health should have been acquired. Your pet's home should be ready and waiting, the cage selected, purchased, and set up. If you fail to do this in advance, you may find yourself trying to fit a stubborn perch in the cage, wondering where to locate the water font and food cups, or discovering that the cage won't fit where you thought it would and having to find another place for it. Should your preparations not be complete when the cockatiel arrives, it will have to remain in its small transport box—not that this will cause harm, but it will be much better if any problems relating to the cage set-up and its location have been worked out in advance.

An early consideration should be the location of the cage. Ideally, one should choose a room often frequented by the bird's keeper and other people, since cockatiels are very sociable birds. The bird's home should be placed where it will receive attention; a room where the family often congregates is preferred to a bedroom. A great deal of thought should be given to the placement of the cage because a bird's environment is very important to its continued health and well being. Cockatiels, like most birds, are easily frightened, so they must be given the opportunity to see when people are approaching. The best height for a cage is at eye level, since birds may feel threatened by any movement from above. This is because birds of prey usually approach from above, and your pet will instinctively fear such movements. The cage should be kept in a location free of drafts. Other hazards are fumes of any type, dry air, smoky areas, and high room temperatures. Cockatiels also need to be in a well-lit spot. However, they must not be exposed to bright sunlight for any length of time. Sudden fluctuations in room temperature should also be avoided. As a general rule, if you are comfortable in a given location, your cockatiel will be also. A good place for a cage would be one where there is plenty of light, no drafts, and where the bird is able to observe activity around it.

Cage Design

A number of considerations go into selecting an appropriate cage, so the matter should be given careful thought. Since cockatiels are hardy birds having a normal life expectancy of more than a decade, a small amount of time spent choosing the cage will be a worthwhile investment. Visits to pet shops will verify that there are many different cages to choose from. Only a few models are really functional and meet the needs of their prospective occupants. Your pet dealer can often give sensible advice about the advantages and disadvantages of the many cage designs that are on the market. Since you will find cages in all manner of styles, materials, and prices, it's best to consider your choice from a practical viewpoint. This means practical not only from your point of view, but also from that of the cockatiel.

A number of cages are immediately appealing; you think they would look nice with a bird inside, or they would fit in with your decor. But it turns out that some of these cages do not make good enclosures for a cockatiel, and some will become an annoyance to you because they're so difficult to clean. Happily, there are enough cages attractively designed that will suit both the cockatiel and its keeper for a long while.

Consider the cage from the cockatiel's point of view. In time, the bird will come to regard the cage as its home, its territory. A cockatiel that spends most of its life in a cage must have ample opportunity for exercise, and it will often be eager to leave the cage for movement and companion-

A suitable cockatiel cage is one that is metal (wooden cages will be chewed to pieces), large and roomy (birds need to exercise their wings and move around), and that has horizontal wires (climbing urges must be satisfied).

Cockatiels enjoy freedom outside of their cages (*above*), but unless your pet is tame and can be easily retrieved, it makes sense to keep it confined to its own home (*below*).

ship. But eventually the bird will want to return—to eat, nap, or just to be in a place where it feels secure. This "homing" behavior may prove to be helpful once your cockatiel has become tame. For example: you will probably decide the bird should be allowed to fly around the room. When a bird recognizes its cage as home, only a little effort is usually sufficient to encourage the bird to return to it. This sense of home is easily reinforced by feeding it only in its cage. It is also wise to keep your hands out of the cage as much as possible. The idea is to foster the bird's sense that the cage belongs to it alone.

When considering the size of the cage one should remember that cockatiels are powerful fliers and creatures native to wide, open spaces; therefore, they should have a roomy cage. The size recommended for larger parrots is preferred. Generally, larger cages are more expensive, but they're better. On the other hand, a bird that will be allowed out of its cage a good deal of the time can do with a smaller one. The main reason to purchase the largest cage you can afford is to ensure that the bird gets enough exercise to keep it healthy. Exercise is important to a bird having to spend most of its time in a relatively small cage. Your cockatiel's cage should be large enough to allow it to stand straight, extend its wings, and stretch, without any part of its body touching the cage. If the cage is not of adequate size, wing and tail feathers will constantly brush against the sides of the cage or stick out between the bars. Frayed and damaged feathers, or a dirty, bedraggled bird will be the result of placing your pet in a cage that is too small for it. Cockatiels are active birds that will make use of all the space you provide for them.

The over-all shape of the cage hasn't been discussed so far. It seems that many people find round cages attractive and decorative. But it's not so obvious that the birds that live inside do. The tall cylindrical cages seem to have little to recommend them for cockatiels. Many bird keepers have concluded that birds prefer rectangular cages. Your cockatiel will probably be happier in a rectangular enclosure in a corner of the room, a bit more snug and cozy than it might be otherwise. Stick to simple shapes and designs. If the sides of the cage extend beyond the base, you can expect feathers, droppings, and seed to be spread over a wider area.

It goes without saying that a better-built but more expensive cage will be a better investment than a cheaper one. Another reason to evaluate durability is the fact that cockatiels like to chew. Thus, a cage with wooden bars is decidedly impractical. Since cockatiels enjoy chewing and gnawing, give them toys to gnaw on.

The ideal cage for a pet cockatiel is all metal, or plastic and metal. Standard heavy parrot wire is preferred to the thinner wire used for budgerigar cages. Most wire cages available today are plated, not painted, which is good, since paint will chip and the cockatiel may gnaw at it. Additionally, most wire cages are easy to clean and should give many years of service. Construction materials to be avoided are wood, including bamboo and wicker. While these materials may be quite attractive, they are entirely impractical for cockatiels that will gnaw upon soft woods and thoroughly enjoy doing so.

In choosing a wire cage it's better if the wiring is horizontal rather than vertical, on at least two sides of the cage. Horizontal wiring will allow the cockatiel to climb around more easily. While it's true that cockatiels are able to lead healthy lives in cages with vertical wiring, it may be a bit more difficult for them to climb around. Horizontal wiring may encourage your bird to exercise.

If the cage has horizontal wiring, vertical wires, or both, it's a good idea to be sure the bird's head will not fit between the bars. If it is able to force its head between the bars, the bird may strangle itself.

Now consider the base of the cage. Old-fashioned cages had a very shallow base, sometimes only an inch high. Cer-

A hand-tame Lutino (*above*) spends time out of its cage perched on its owner's outstretched finger. The bird below has progressed a step further in its social development with humans: it is learning to mimic words.

Cockatiels enjoy perching in high places; therefore, it is not uncommon to find them sitting atop their owner's shoulders.

tainly that let you see everything the bird might be doing, but in time this seemed less important in view of the effort required to keep the area around the cage clean of seed hulls and feathers. Cages were then designed with shallow bases but with panes of glass (later, plastic) fitted along the wire sides. These "seed guards" were something else to clean, and the glass ones got broken now and then. Today, the current trend in cage design is to have a deep base, thereby eliminating the need for seed guards. If you're starting to worry about this, or if you're one of those people who dislike messes so much that neither deep bases nor seed guards will be enough, your pet shop has available strips of clear plastic—again called seed guards—that will wrap around almost any cage.

The bases of most cages you are likely to find incorporate a removable tray. Some trays are shallow, some deep. While the deeper trays may be preferred, one argument in favor of the shallow tray is that it mandates frequent emptying and cleaning, which is all to the good as far as the cockatiel is concerned.

Another feature to be considered is the cage door. The preferred door will have a double catch—one to fasten it open and one to securely fasten it closed—so that your inquisitive pet will not learn to pop it open with its beak. The opening should be large enough for the bird to pass through it easily, and there should be adequate space for your hand to reach inside to perform the necessary chores. All too often a prospective cockatiel owner purchases an oversize budgerigar cage thinking that his bird will have adequate space, only to find the opening in the cage too small for the larger bird.

The door should be constructed so that it will remain open while the bird is out of the cage, in the event it wants to return. A nice feature is a door that is hinged on the bottom; when open it becomes a landing perch, making it easy for your cockatiel to return to the cage.

An appropriate cage for a single cockatiel (*above*). One nice feature is the cage door which opens downward so that the cockatiel can exit and enter easily. In contrast, the flight below accommodates several birds.

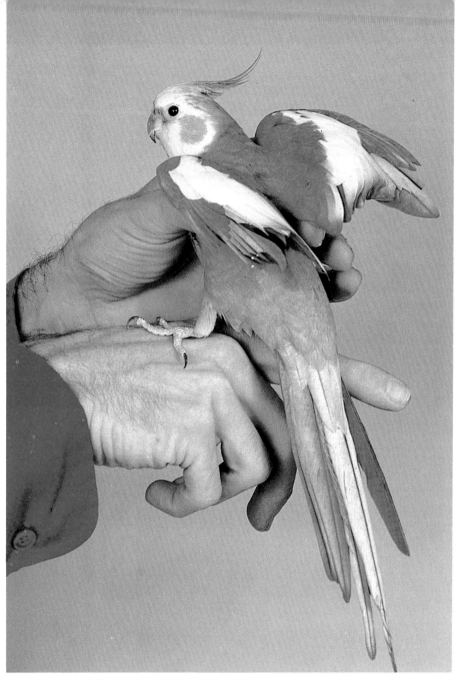

The cockatiel above has just had its left wing clipped. The same bird (*facing page*) preens its feathers while the handler trims the bird's claws.

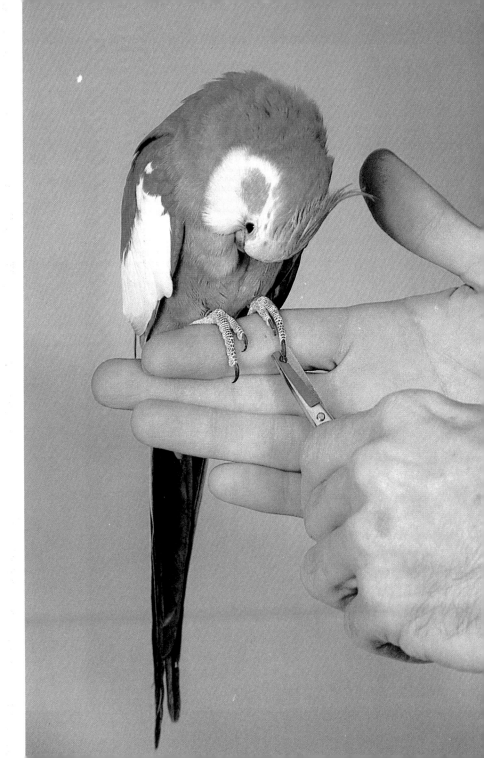

Furnishing the Cage

The arrangement of the cage is almost as important as its construction. It must be easy to clean; both you and the bird should be able to reach the seed and water containers with ease. There should be at least three perches, and the cage design should provide enough flexibility to arrange them in a hygienic fashion. Positioning of the perches is important; they should not be placed in locations where the bird's droppings can foul the food or water. This is an *essential* of cage arrangement. Perches should allow easy access to food and water, and one should be near the top of the cage.

It is best that the perches be of different diameters so that the bird's grasp will vary. If at all possible, the perches that come with the cage should be replaced with natural branches, from fruit, elm, hazelnut, willow, alder, or hawthorn trees, for example. This will not only make for perches of varying diameters but will also provide something for the bird to gnaw on. It should be noted that a cockatiel's feet are considerably larger than those of a canary or budgerigar; consequently their perches should be about ¾ inch in diameter. Constant nibbling by the cockatiel as well as scraping and cleaning by the owner necessitate somewhat frequent replacement of the perches.

There are a number of other aspects to be considered when picking out a cage for your cockatiel. It might not be possible to find the ideal cage, but the closer you can come to finding all of the desirable features, the easier will be your job of caring for the bird.

Some manufacturers equip their cages with fitted food cups that can be serviced from outside the cage. While this is a handy feature, it is not too important, as other types of food cups can be located anywhere in the cage without limiting your cage arrangement. If accessories supplied with the cage, such as perches and seed cups, do not meet your needs or those of the bird, substitute items are available. The substitutes may be more easily cleaned, installed, or filled. You may wish to consider installation of a tube drinker. While a slight additional expense is involved, most owners feel the convenience to be well worth it. Tube drinkers are not fouled as easily as open water cups, and they hold a larger supply. While it's still best to change the water daily, the larger capacity will allow you to leave your cockatiel unattended for a couple of days.

A modern, well-stocked pet shop may display an unbelievable array of attractive accessories, toys, and other items for the comfort and joy of your bird. It is often difficult, even irresistible, to avoid the temptation to purchase more than one needs. The only items initially essential are perches, food and water vessels, and a cuttlebone. After your bird has settled into its new home, you may wish to acquire some well constructed toys to provide both enjoyment and exercise for your pet.

When purchasing a cage, think about a cover for it. It is not an absolute necessity, but a cover may be useful. Cockatiels do not see well in the dark and often become startled or frightened at strange sounds. It is best to completely cover a cage at night to avoid having the bird thrash around in the cage and injure itself. Covers also keep the bird cozy and free from subtle drafts while it's sleeping. Quiet and darkness are more conducive to sleep. The bird soon learns that when the cover is on, it is bedtime, and it will settle down for the night. Cage covers are also useful in quieting the bird, as some birds can become quite annoying with their constant chattering or talking.

Cockatiels that are allowed out of their cages naturally will take flight and explore their surroundings. To prevent a bird from unknowingly flying into a closed window and possibly injuring itself, carry the bird over to the window and let it perch on the window frame; this way, the bird will become familiar with the hard glass surface.

Cockatiel Care

Whenever you are thinking of purchasing something for your cockatiel, whether it be the cage, a toy, or a food treat, be certain to evaluate it for safety, just as you would something that will be used by a child. Some bird toys have metal or plastic parts that will not stand up to a cockatiel's beak. Cockatiels have been injured by toys they've been able to tear apart.

Preventing Accidents

When you are ready to allow your cockatiel outside its cage, remember to consider the mischief it may get into. A bird should not be allowed the freedom of a room unless someone is there to watch it. For example, doors and windows should be closed. Windows can be treacherous: your cockatiel may be unfamiliar with them and try to fly on through. Be sure to remove anything you think may be dangerous to your pet.

It is generally agreed that their natural curiosity makes cockatiels somewhat accident-prone. If your bird is to be allowed any degree of freedom out of its cage, a great deal of care must be taken to ensure a safe environment. More often than not, the owner of a cockatiel is at fault when there is an unfortunate mishap. It's the owner's responsibility to foresee the danger to the bird and take the necessary steps to prevent an accident. The kinds of trouble a bird can get into are unbelievable; it takes a great deal of foresight and imagination to prevent your pet from harming itself. Cockatiels, like small children, should never be allowed their freedom without giving thought to hazards that may be present. They should never be left unsupervised for even a short time.

Can you imagine a cockatiel drowning in a pitcher of water, being shut inside a refrigerator, being caught by a pet cat, or flying into a mirror and breaking its neck? Stranger accidents than these have happened to cockatiels, and they can happen to *your* bird if you are not careful when the bird is allowed some freedom. The age-old phrase, "An ounce of prevention is worth a pound of cure," is most appropriate here.

Preventing Illness

As with accidents, illness is best dealt with in terms of prevention. So far as infectious diseases are concerned, the key to prevention is cleanliness. The bird's surroundings—cage and play area—should be kept scrupulously clean. Generally, cockatiels are tidy birds, so cleaning up after them is not much of a problem. It takes only a few moments to do the job, and your bird certainly deserves a clean environment. It is best to clean the cage each day, either in the morning or the evening. Cleaning every other day is an absolute minimum. The cage tray should be cleaned and the paper liner removed and replaced. A regular cleaning schedule must be maintained, not only for the tray but also for the perches, food and water containers, toys, playground, and the cage cover. The water font should be cleansed daily, while the other parts of the cage and objects in and around it should receive attention once a week.

On a monthly basis everything should be thoroughly cleaned. The scrubbing should be done with hot water containing a strong disinfectant, followed by hot and cold water rinses. After being cleaned, all items must be carefully dried. Perches may be either washed or scraped; if washed, let them dry completely before putting them back in the cage.

Bathing

Washing is fine for the cage and accessories, and it's good for your cockatiel too. It's best if the cockatiel does it itself, if it takes baths regularly.

Although cockatiels originate in open, semi-arid regions, they have been observed bathing and splashing about on the edges of small pools in stream beds. In the wild, they are naturally "bathed" by rain showers, so they seem to particularly enjoy being showered by falling spray or rain. When the bird preens, you will see that it occasionally obtains a bit of oil from a gland located near the base of the tail. The oil is rubbed over the feathers by the beak.

To provide your bird with an opportunity to bathe, a shallow bowl, heavy enough to prevent accidental tipping, can be used for a bird bath. Those made of red clay, available from garden and pet shops, are ideal. It is not necessary to leave the bowl in the cage at all times; it can be placed in the cage every few days for about a half hour. Room-temperature water should be used in the bath.

We do not advocate the often-mentioned practice of allowing your bird to bathe or shower in the kitchen sink. Even though cockatiels seem to naturally gravitate to a running faucet and attempt to shower underneath it, once they learn to do this, there is the possibility they will attempt to steal a bath when the water is unusually hot and thus be tragically killed.

Alternatively, you may want to try spraying your cockatiel with room-temperature water. Garden sprayers used for misting plants are ideal for this purpose. One should spray with caution as some birds may be frightened by the spray until they become used to it. Baths serve to stimulate preening and improve the appearance of the plumage.

Throughout this book, suggestions have been given to help you to know about the essentials of cockatiel care. The described regimen, recommendations about cleanliness, and comments regarding feeding have not been casually

Perching and climbing up the sides of the cage occupy much of the cockatiel's time (*facing page*). All manner of perches appeal to cockatiels, including a colorful plastic dish rack (*above*) or the edge of a glass pie plate (*below*). The glass dish filled with tepid water serves as a nice bird bath!

suggested—they are *absolutely essential* if you are to maintain a healthy bird. When a cockatiel is well fed on a balanced diet of fresh, nutritional foods; when it has been housed in a sanitary environment that is maintained with a carefully followed cleaning schedule; when it is kept free of dampness, drafts, and other harmful conditions in the area where it is housed; and when given sufficient exercise, you will find it is likely to suffer from very few ailments. Under such conditions, in fact, illness is a rare occurrence. It is far better to avoid sickness by keeping a bird under optimal living conditions than to try to cure it once it has become ill. Furthermore, it is not always possible to cure an ailing bird; this is particularly true if the ailment is either incorrectly diagnosed or recognized too late for treatment to be effective.

First Aid

Whether your cockatiel has an accident or becomes ill, immediate, correct treatment is essential. Although there are a few relatively simple health problems that can be dealt with, and in spite of the fact that there are some first-aid measures that are generally beneficial, the safest and most advisable course of action is to consult an experienced veterinarian. Since veterinary physicians experienced in the treatment of birds are sometimes difficult to find, you may wish to seek one out in advance. This should be done while your bird is still healthy—the "ounce of prevention" again.

Since it's not possible to adequately cover here all the problems that may afflict a pet cockatiel, only some first-aid measures will be discussed. To further prepare yourself for eventualities, it is recommended that you read one of the books available on this aspect of bird care.

Accidents often result in bleeding. In all cases, it's imperative to stop the bleeding at once. Styptic powder and pressure will usually do the job. If bleeding persists, or if the wound is so large as to require suturing, or if healing is not apparent in a few days, then veterinary attention is necessary.

Another frequent result of accidents is a broken bone. The important thing is to immobilize the bird, by wrapping it in a towel, for example, to prevent further damage. Professional help offers the best chance of successfully repairing the fracture and averting lameness.

Burns should be flushed with cold water, then dried gently. If your cockatiel has been exposed to toxic fumes, remove the bird to fresh air immediately. The correct response to poisoning depends on what the poison is; call your veterinarian or local poison-control center immediately.

Any of the foregoing, as well as other trauma, may cause your cockatiel to go into shock. If your bird is immobile, breathing rapidly, with feathers fluffed, you should suspect shock. It is imperative to conserve the bird's body heat until you can get veterinary attention. Wrap it in a towel, cover the cage, or use a heat lamp. Be careful not to change the bird's position abruptly, as this may cause death. Remember, shock is serious. Careful, gentle handling of ill or injured birds is mandatory, as shock or its aggravation is always possible.

Injuries resulting from accidents have one good feature: they are usually easy to spot. More insidious are diseases that have a slow and subtle onset. Birds may in fact be ill long before they show it; the only way to deal with this is to observe your cockatiel daily, to be sure you don't miss the earliest signs of illness. You should quickly recognize that something is amiss should the bird exhibit ruffled feathers, loss of appetite, listlessness, excessive thirst, discharge from the eyes and nostrils, watery and discolored droppings, or other more obvious signs of illness. Generally speaking, the puffed, huddled, sick appearance is obvious and easily recognized. A sick bird will often sleep with both feet widely spread on the perch; on the other hand, resting on one

Under adult supervision, children are capable of taming cockatiels.

foot, with the other drawn up, is a sign of health. Closing eyelids is another danger signal.

If your cockatiel shows any of these signs, the first step is to warm it. Depending on the cage, the temperature inside can be increased by covering it with a towel and placing it on a heating pad. Heat lamps and ordinary incandescent light bulbs can also be used, though less successfully. The temperature inside the cage should be kept between 85 and 90 F. Some improvement should be noted within a few hours. During this time, be careful to notice whether your cockatiel is eating normally. If you do not find evident improvement in the bird's condition by the next day, it's time to consult your vet.

On the whole, bird diseases tend to progress rapidly. This has to do with your cockatiel's small size and high rate of metabolism. If you value your pet, it's best when illness does occur to seek professional help immediately. It's too often the case that stop-gap home remedies are beside the point and only make treatment specific to the illness more difficult when it is undertaken—if it isn't by then too late.

You can take courage from the fact that a cockatiel kept singly is not exposed to the main avenue of disease: other birds. There is only a slight chance that illness can be introduced via food or supplies. If a few months have passed since you acquired your cockatiel and it appears as healthy as ever, you can look forward to an illness-free future.

This consideration applies as well to parasites, such as mites and lice. If the cockatiel you purchase is free of them, it will not get them spontaneously thereafter. When you purchase your cockatiel, ask the seller to make sure that it is free of parasites.

Just as you looked your cockatiel over closely when you bought it, you should do the same whenever you have it in hand for grooming purposes. If you happen to be clipping claws, take the time to give your cockatiel something of a physical examination.

In case you don't recall clearly how the seller handled your cockatiel when you bought it, it may be helpful to describe how a cockatiel may be restrained.

Quick movements are to be avoided. When handling a bird, be as gentle as possible at all times. A cockatiel should be held with the thumb and first finger controlling the head. If the bird attempts to bite you, placing your thumb under the beak will control its movement. When holding the bird in your hand, be sure that you do not restrict respiration. Also, do not press against the nostrils or eyes.

While holding a bird for examination can be done by one person, unless you have a particularly tame bird, two pairs of hands are preferred for trimming. One person holds the bird, watching its respiration and holding it still. The individual holding the bird should neither pull its head nor push it into the body. The bird's body should not be allowed to twist. The bird should be supported on one's lap or on a towel-covered counter. While it is being carefully held, a second person should do the trimming.

Usually it's not strictly necessary to trim the claws of an active cockatiel, as normal climbing and perching activity serves to keep them sufficiently worn down. If the claws become too long, they curve back in such a way that the cockatiel will find it difficult to grip the perch. Specially made bird-claw clippers should be used to snip off the tip of the claw. There is a dark blood vessel along the inside of the claw, which may be seen by holding the claw up to a light source. Be sure to avoid clipping into this blood vessel. Should there be an accident, with resultant bleeding, apply styptic powder with light pressure.

As an active, healthy bird will not have beak problems, trimming the beak is rarely necessary. If a problem with the beak develops, try to determine the cause, instead of just trimming and forgetting that a problem exists. A beak conditioner, cuttlebone, and mineral block will often prevent such difficulties. If your bird should develop a misshapen

The claws of an active, healthy bird usually wear down by themselves due to normal climbing and perching activities (*above*). Whenever you need to handle your cockatiel (*facing page*), spend some time examining the bird. This quick physical examination should include, among other things, an evaluation of the bird's claws; if they have become too long, clipping may be necessary.

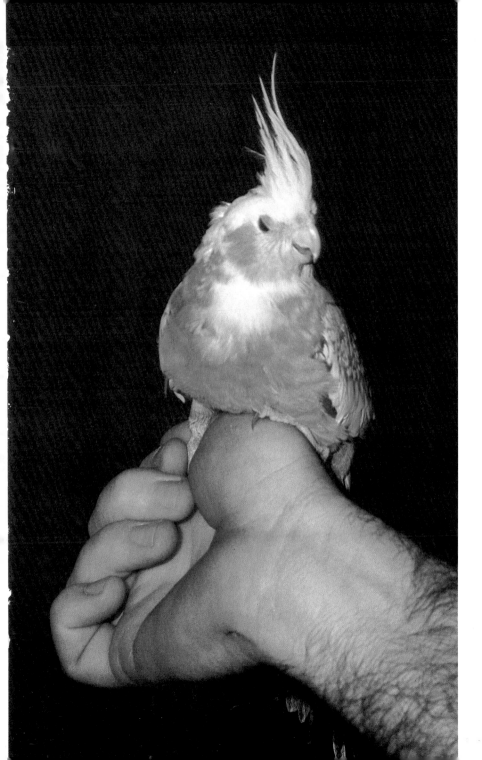

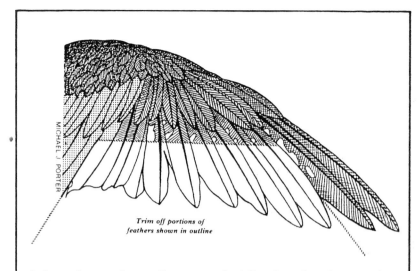

Trim off portions of feathers shown in outline

It is not imperative to clip your cockatiel's wings, but the procedure does make taming the bird easier, since it prevents the bird from flying away from you. One popular method of wing clipping involves trimming approximately ten of the primary flight feathers and leaving the two feathers at the end of the wing uncut, as illustrated here.

or overgrown beak, it will have to be trimmed back to its normal shape. If this is not done, the bird will have difficulty cracking seeds and may not be able to eat properly. It also becomes almost impossible for the bird to preen its feathers if the beak is deformed. After the beak has been trimmed—with scissors or clippers, whichever's appropriate—the edges can be smoothed with a nail file or emery board. In trimming the beak you are attempting to return it to a natural configuration. The same procedure is followed for both the top and bottom parts of the beak. When the trimming is finished, check to see that the beak closes correctly. As with the claws, the beak contains a blood supply; since this is extensive, extreme care should be taken when cutting. Some bird owners are hesitant to attempt to trim a beak, preferring to engage professional assistance—this is a wise attitude.

Many experts in bird taming advocate trimming the wing feathers to restrict flight. This will prevent the bird from getting away from you, making taming far easier. "Trimming the wings," as it's often called, means cutting only *part* of the wing *feathers*. It's usually necessary to trim the feathers of only one wing, the purpose being to unbalance the cockatiel's flight. With a particularly energetic bird, it may be necessary to trim both wings.

Before starting, look for any "blood feathers"; they should not be clipped. A blood feather, or pin feather, is one that has not finished growing. Part of the feather is still enclosed in its sheath, which has a blood supply. If cut, the sheath may bleed considerably. Should you accidentally cut a blood feather, styptic powder should be applied to stop the bleeding.

Again, it's best to have two persons for this procedure: one to hold and one to clip. The two feathers at the end of the wing are usually left uncut for the sake of appearance. The adjacent ten feathers should at first be cut halfway from wing to tip. If this proves insufficient, the feathers may be trimmed further, so long as at least one-half inch of feather is left extending from the wing.

The initial taming of a cockatiel should be accomplished by the family member who will be primarily responsible for it. Later, other relatives and friends can spend time with the bird.

Taming
and
Training

Before beginning to outline a program, or schedule, and indicating techniques for taming and training, some general advice is in order. Fundamentally, the taming process boils down to allowing your cockatiel to become accustomed to *you*.

This means that you alone should be the person doing the taming of your bird. Once the bird has become tame and has gained a great deal of confidence in you, it can be introduced to other members of the family, perhaps even to friends or visitors. In the beginning, however, others in the family should be asked to stay away from it. You will have to explain the reason for this enforced solitude if a family feud is to be avoided. Others who are interested in the bird will have to be told they will have an opportunity to become acquainted with it at a later time. Your bird must become totally tame with you before you can begin to think about its being tame with strangers. The key to all of this is frequent contact—try to spend as much time as possible with your new pet. The more attention you are able to give your cockatiel, the more tame it will become. It is also true that once your bird is tame, if it then has sufficient contact with your family, it will likely be tame with them as well.

What to Expect
There are some clues as to what you can expect of a bird. If a young cockatiel reacts favorably to being handled when you buy it, you can expect that it will be reasonably easy to tame. If you happen to be able to find a cockatiel that already knows a word or two, it is certainly reasonable to

expect that the bird's vocabulary can be developed further without much difficulty.

The variety of experiences any bird has had before you obtain it will, without a doubt, influence its behavior. At least to some degree, the cockatiel has begun to form its personality by the time you acquire it. If the bird you have selected behaves calmly while the pet dealer trims its wing feathers and claws, you may rest assured that the bird has already experienced gentle handling by others.

Just as observation of the cockatiel you've chosen will give you an idea of what to hope for from it, so should observation be the basis for deciding how soon you should begin training your bird. There are two schools of thought about this: one suggests that taming should begin immediately, as soon as you get your cockatiel home; the other believes you should let your bird get accustomed to its new home for a while, perhaps even a few days. The strategy you employ with your cockatiel should be determined by what you are able to tell from its behavior.

Any cockatiel you're likely to obtain has spent its entire life in captivity. It has always been around people, more or less. Thus, human handling will result in little stress, compared to what may be experienced by a wild-caught bird. Similarly, you can expect that your cockatiel will not be severely affected by being moved from one location to another. But it will still take some time for the cockatiel to adjust to its new surroundings. Many bird trainers see an opportunity here; they advise undertaking taming immediately because it seems the bird's disorientation in a new location makes it more amenable to learning. If you wish to follow this course, you should arrange to bring your cockatiel home early enough in the day so that you can have your first taming session as soon as the bird is taken out of the transport box. The first day the bird is at home, spend as much time as you can with it. Watch the bird carefully; if there is any sign of stress, if the bird seems unwell, or if the taming is not proceeding satisfactorily, it's best to put the bird in its cage and wait for another time. Should this happen, you will in effect be forced to follow the second approach mentioned, beginning taming at some later time.

The tame-later approach certainly minimizes any unnecessary stress to the cockatiel, making the transition to a new home as easy as possible. You also have a good opportunity to observe the bird and to be sure it is doing well. There is always the possibility that the cockatiel will have had a difficult time during the trip home.

A Flexible Program

In addition to the fact that there are two schools of thought about how soon you should begin taming, there is also a difference of opinion about every other point in training birds. The conclusions that may be reached from all this are clear: there's more than one way to accomplish any training task, and no one way is entirely superior to another. You will have to decide which methods best suit you, and the methods will depend on your ability, your situation, and, most important of all, your cockatiel.

There's an encouraging side to this lengthy discussion. No single aspect, in the entire process of taming and training, is critical to its overall success. Just as to start taming later, instead of immediately, does not spell failure, neither do two training sessions a day instead of four. On the other hand, recognize that while no single step is critical to your success, the aggregate is. You won't end up with the kind of performance you want if you find yourself fudging a little every step of the way.

The Taming Area

Taming your cockatiel is the *first* step to be accomplished. All efforts at taming should be conducted in the same, distraction-free area. Taming is best accomplished in a confined area, so the bird cannot get away from you. Thus, it

Cockatiels, like many parrots, enjoy climbing up and down toy ladders, but those made of wood are apt to be chewed.

A tame bird that feels secure with its owner probably won't mind a little push as it sits happily on its swing (*above*). Toys provide stimulation for a singly-kept cockatiel; however, the bird also needs some human companionship (*below*).

may be possible to tame the bird in its cage, but the success of this approach depends on how wild, or territorial, your cockatiel is and how much space within the cage it has to avoid you. For example, the cockatiel may decide to retreat to a high corner, and you'll have to twist your arm through the door repeatedly in attempts to get your hand—or a taming stick—close to the bird. All things considered, taming will proceed more smoothly if both you and the bird have room to maneuver. For this reason—and the fact that your cockatiel is likely to be more aggressive in what it considers to be its own territory—it is preferable to tame your cockatiel outside its cage. A small room then becomes the choice for a taming area. If it's necessary to conduct the taming sessions in a larger room, you can use some kind of sheet to enclose a convenient corner. The taming area should be a place where you and the bird can move freely, within comfortable limits.

Since your cockatiel will be unable to fly because its feathers are trimmed, it's best to work on the floor. This way the cockatiel is less likely to injure itself. It will take a little time before the bird realizes it can no longer fly. Even then it's possible that it may still launch itself into the air. Feather clipping may not eliminate the problem of chasing the bird around the room, but it's imperative that you keep in mind the danger of falls, so long as the bird is unable to fly.

In order to ensure that the attention of the bird is completely focused on you during taming and training, all distractions must be removed from the taming area. Mirrors should be covered or removed. Work with the bird as often as possible, and use short lessons to keep its attention. The more brief sessions you are able to work into your bird's day, the faster it will learn.

Scheduling Sessions

This brings up the matter of scheduling training sessions. It should be clear to you that training will take a reasonable amount of time. Those who are most successful at it are the ones who are able to spend enough time with their cockatiels to accomplish the task. You already know that frequency of contact with your bird is an all-important factor. It is generally accepted that many short sessions each day will give better results than one or two longer sessions. Each training session should last from ten to fifteen minutes. Several sessions should be held each day. Repetition is the key to taming a cockatiel.

Even if you are a very busy person, you should schedule a minimum of two sessions with your cockatiel every day, more whenever possible. The more sessions you are able to schedule, the greater the likelihood that you will be successful. The obvious times for taming and training are in the morning and in the evening. As with any other task, the sooner you start to work with your bird, and the harder you work at it, the more likely it is that you will get the desired results. Just remember that the results cannot be guaranteed in advance; there are far too many variables. It is a fact that some cockatiels will become more tame than others; that some will be good performers and others won't; and that some develop relatively large vocabularies, while many do not. These observations serve to underline the fact that every cockatiel is an individual!

A Cockatiel's Moods

You will be much more successful in taming and training if you pay close attention to your cockatiel's moods. A cardinal rule in bird keeping is to *observe the bird*. Try to put yourself into its feathers and imagine what it is experiencing. While we certainly understand that a cockatiel is not a little human being and cannot be expected to behave as we do, it is most important that we remember that the bird is not a wind-up toy; it deserves attention. As you work with your bird, keep in mind that its day is pretty much like yours. There are times when it wants to make noise, times

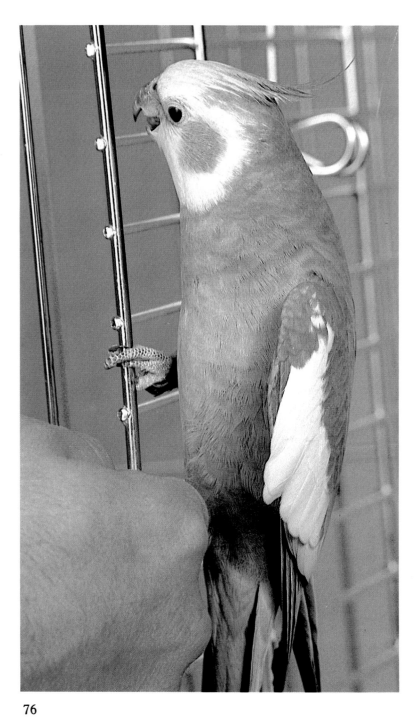

Cockatiels enjoy climbing inside and out of their cages (*facing page*).
They also enjoy spray millet (*above*), and this treat can be offered as a
reward for good behavior.

when it wants to take a nap, and times when it is physically active. When the cockatiel wants to play with its toys or fly about its play area, these are the times to teach tricks. However, this mood is not compatible with training it to talk.

Although every cockatiel has a wide range of moods, just as humans do, the range will be different from bird to bird. The experiences of a friend with his or her bird may be somewhat different from those you have with your cockatiel. Each bird has its own personality. If you haven't had experience with a number of birds, this won't be obvious; but after looking at a cage full of cockatiels in a pet shop, the variations in activity level will be readily apparent.

In general, the periods when your cockatiel is most excited will not be productive for taming or training. Indeed, you may get better results in taming if you work with your bird when it is in a less active, quieter mood. The bird is likely to be more tractable at these times.

If some of your training or taming sessions should turn out to be failures, there is always the possibility this may have happened because the bird simply wasn't in the right mood for the activity you had in mind.

Besides paying close attention to your cockatiel's behavior, it's also essential that you watch your own. How you behave whenever you are around a bird is important.

Owner's Behavior

From the moment you bring it home you are in a position to win its friendship. This does not mean that you are required to begin working with your bird at once. It does mean, however, that everything that happens in the cockatiel's vicinity will have some effect on it. It becomes very important for you to be aware of what you are doing in the presence of the cockatiel.

When working near the bird, make every attempt to move purposefully; quick, unexpected movements may frighten it and delay the formation of the bond you are attempting to foster between the bird and yourself.

The way you talk to the bird is also important. It makes little difference to the cockatiel if you are talking to it or to someone across the room. Your voice should always be quiet, gentle, calm, and reassuring.

Taming is nothing more than getting your pet accustomed to you, to climb upon your finger, to allow you to take it in and out of its cage.

Hand Taming

Almost by definition, when we think of a tame bird, we usually think of a bird that will perch on one's finger. Strictly speaking, such a bird is *hand tame*. Tameness properly understood is a matter of degree. Wild birds are described as tame if they allow you to approach within a few feet before flying away. At the other extreme are cage birds that will allow you to handle their plumage and will lie motionless in your hands. Not all cockatiels will come to permit this sort of handling, so don't be surprised if yours doesn't.

It's worth considering what your hands represent to a bird. It's not the nature of birds to be inclined toward much physical contact. In many species, the mere fact that they press their bodies together while perching seems remarkable enough to deserve comment, since most birds prefer to keep some space between themselves and their fellows. (It's worth noting that if you want something to fondle, you'll be more satisfied with a dog or a cat.) Unless a bird becomes accustomed to human hands during its infancy, its first experience with hands will be as an unwanted restraint. Moreover, even many hand-raised birds, as they mature, will be less inclined to be held.

It is not possible to avoid instances in which a bird will experience hands as a restraint; claw clipping and physical examinations will be necessary from time to time. One way

Some cockatiel owners prefer to start with stick training rather than hand training since cage birds are used to perching on sticks of various sorts (*above*). The T-stick (*below*) is also a useful piece of training equipment. This bird (*facing page*) has learned a new trick: it is learning to climb a chain.

to prevent having the bird make negative associations with your hands is to wear thin gloves on these occasions.

Many people contemplating taming a bird are worried about being bitten. With a cockatiel this is a valid concern, as they can inflict painful bites, although they do little damage. Birds bite because they are frightened or nervous. Biting will become a serious behavior problem if the bird is constantly uncomfortable in its surroundings. If your cockatiel bites, the only response you should make is a loud "no!" If it persists in biting, discontinue the taming session, and wait until the bird is more mellow.

When working with your cockatiel, be careful that you aren't mistaking what the cockatiel may be trying to do with its beak. Cockatiels, like other parrots, use their beaks in ways that many other birds do not. Biting is a means of defense, of course, but even a tame cockatiel will at times nibble on your finger. This behavior can be understood because of their inclination to gnaw; they also use their beaks to move about. Notice how your cockatiel employs its beak. Very often, before moving to an unfamiliar perch, a cockatiel will test it with its beak. When you first present a finger to your cockatiel, if it reaches out slowly with an open beak, it's probably trying to determine if your finger is a secure perch. Bites are usually delivered swiftly.

Taming with Sticks

If your cockatiel is inclined to bite, then it is recommended that you begin taming it by using sticks, instead of offering your hand. As with many other aspects of cockatiel taming that have already been noted, there is some question about the use of sticks, whether these be dowels, such as those used for perches, or small branches from trees. Cockatiels are smart enough to know the difference between sticks and hands and to recognize that sticks are held in your hand. Some trainers look upon teaching a cockatiel to step on and off a stick as the first stage in the process of hand-taming.

Others believe that stick training is unnecessary and can be eliminated entirely. The latter have obviously not been dissuaded by a painful bite from the cockatiel's strong beak. Stick training is a good beginning because the cockatiel is accustomed to perching on sticks. Should your bird be one of the wilder ones, taming will probably proceed more smoothly if you start with stick training.

Perhaps a more interesting argument is that training your bird to step onto a stick held by you may prove to be very useful. For example, if your cockatiel gets itself into a position that is difficult to reach, it's very handy to have the bird step onto a stick so that you can bring it within reach. In any event, it's a good idea to have a T-stick around, for they have many uses. The T-stick consists of two dowels, of an appropriate size, joined together in the shape of the letter *T*; the handle should be at least two feet long.

The Taming Program

When you're ready to begin your first taming session, move either the transport box or the cage into the taming area. Open the box and the bird will soon come out. If the bird is in its cage, it may not venture out if you merely open the door. But if you remove the bottom and turn the cage on its side, this will allow you to approach the bird.

Should the bird react wildly as you approach it, do not jerk away. If you make this mistake, the cockatiel will soon learn how to keep you at bay. With the bird on the floor, take the stick (or your finger) and move it in front of the bird until it touches the bird's abdomen, above and in front of its feet. You are attempting to get the cockatiel to step up onto the stick. You want it to stay perched on the stick as you hold it. If you move the stick, the cockatiel will probably jump off. This is your cue to present the stick again. The cockatiel must be taught to step onto the stick when it is presented, and to stay there. When this has been accomplished, take a second stick and teach the cockatiel to

This Lutino has just lighted on its owner's hand. It will probably take several taming sessions before the bird becomes accustomed to you and voluntarily sits on your hand.

step up from one to another. As you drill the cockatiel in these maneuvers, it becomes more and more accustomed to your being close to it. Other drills can teach the cockatiel to step from the stick to the T-stick, to a playground, or onto or into its cage, as you like. Stick training can be said to be accomplished when the cockatiel will remain quietly perched on the stick as you stand and move about the taming area.

A stick is one thing but your hand is another. The next stage in taming is this: with your cockatiel perched on a stick, present a finger as you did the second stick. Try to have the cockatiel step from the stick onto your finger. If the bird is very reluctant to do this, go back to drills with sticks alone. Try offering food rewards by hand in the course of the drill; this should have the effect of lessening the bird's fear of your hands. Try a sunflower seed; if that doesn't work, try spray millet. A timid cockatiel may be more inclined to nibble the end of a long spray of millet. With time, you can offer shorter and shorter lengths.

In hand taming, many people are amazed to find that their bird will soon step onto their finger and move quickly onto their arm or even their shoulder. "What success!" they think. Actually, the bird may just be making its escape from those treacherous hands. Successful hand taming means that your cockatiel will be content to remain perched on your hand, not on your shoulder. Drill the bird in perching on your hands by having it step from finger to finger.

Repetition and Reinforcement

By now the importance of drills in each behavior should be obvious. It's desirable that each be mastered before moving onto the next. Subsequent taming sessions should review what has been taught in the previous ones. You will find that all the ways you can handle your cockatiel will come in handy at one time or another.

Provided your cockatiel is willing to accept food from your hands, rewards do seem to hasten learning. Once a bird has become hand-tame, they can certainly be useful in teaching more complicated tricks.

You may wish to also employ verbal commands in the course of your taming exercises. Though a cockatiel will step onto a stick because it is presented, not because you say "Up," the bird can associate the command with the behavior. By further training, "Up" can eventually be used to cue the cockatiel to hop from a perch to a held stick, for example, or to fly from one to the other.

Teaching Tricks

You may be content with the repertoire of tricks your cockatiel is able to teach itself, or you may wish to a take a more active role in its training. You will find that a pet cockatiel, left to its own devices or given an interesting toy, will amaze you with the tricks it can do. A tame cockatiel kept by itself enjoys inventing its own tricks—all the bird needs is a chance to do so. If you want to increase the chances of your cockatiel's keeping itself happily occupied, and at the same time providing you with hours of amusement, go to your local pet shop and pick out a playground. There are a number of designs from which to choose. You will find playgrounds made of metal, wood, or plastic and equipped with swings, perches, ladders, and bells. The variety is almost endless. Purchase a playground that is large enough for a cockatiel; some designed for budgerigars will not accommodate the larger bird. Prices depend on how elaborate the playground is. You are sure to find one that will meet your needs.

Once the playground is placed in an appropriate, carefully selected location, you will find that it affords a means of keeping your cockatiel interested and occupied. It is often convenient to place the playground near the cage. Whenever the bird is allowed out of the cage, it will probably move to the playground and spend a great deal of time amusing itself there. Some of the unexpected advantages of

The cockatiels above and below are obviously very gentle towards their owners. It is important during training to move slowly and speak in a quiet, soothing tone. Stepping from the stick to the finger can be mastered in just a short time (*facing page*).

such a device are that it will keep your cockatiel away from doors and windows and unsafe areas, and it will give the bird a place to perch that is not inconvenient for you. A playground of any type is a worthwhile investment, as it provides endless fun for the bird as well as pleasure for you.

If you choose a more active role in teaching your cockatiel some tricks, it will be helpful to remember that all tricks are based on three simple acts: riding, climbing, and using the beak. If you can teach your bird to do these three things, you will be repaid with an endless display of variations of these three basic acts.

It is helpful to understand that in spite of the fact that cockatiels are intelligent birds, there is a limit to their ability to learn. There is also the fact that they are quite easily distracted. Since animals learn by association, it is necessary to reward proper performance *immediately* so that the bird comes to realize what is expected or (from the bird's viewpoint) what behavior will result in the reward of a treat. If teaching the trick is to be effective, your cockatiel must learn that the reward comes as a result of its correct behavior.

Teaching tricks can be a tedious job; for some people, it may take over a year to teach the most difficult tricks. Before you make the decision to engage in teaching some tricks to your cockatiel, be sure that you have the patience and temperament required for the job. Also decide whether the expenditure of time is worth the result. If you think you can do the job, and you want to, go to it!

Climbing a Ladder. Cockatiels enjoy climbing up and down the sides of their cages. It will not take long for your bird to learn to go up a ladder. If you place the cockatiel on the bottom rung, it may just begin to climb by itself. If not, give the bird a gentle push. Keep pushing if the bird hesitates at any step. Don't let the cockatiel jump off or go only halfway up. It should be taught to climb all the way to the top of the ladder each time. Repeat the process over and over again, rewarding your pet each time it is successful. Keep each session short; also, don't attempt to teach more than one trick at a time.

Rope Climbing. When you have succeeded in having your cockatiel climb a ladder, follow up by teaching it to climb a rope or walk a tightrope. Begin with rope (or chain) thick enough for the bird's grasp. Find a way to make the rope vertical and taut; then place the bird at the bottom and patiently push it up. Once the cockatiel understands what is expected of it, it will climb the rope each time it is put near it. If you do the same with the rope fixed in a horizontal position, the bird will walk your tightrope. Actually, it's probably better to accustom the bird to the horizontal rope first. Be patient; your bird may not pick up these tricks as fast as you'd like, so be sure it is not your fault it is not doing well.

Riding in a Car. One of the easiest tricks is to teach your cockatiel to ride on a small toy car equipped with a perch as you pull the car around. Let the bird become familiar with the toy for a few days. If necessary, show it how to hop onto the perch. With constant repetition, the bird will soon hop onto the perch (or into a toy without a perch) when brought to it.

Pulling a Toy. When you want your bird to pull a toy, just show it what you want it to do. The bird will soon learn that something is expected when a toy or other object is placed in its beak. Since cockatiels are attracted to shiny things, a metal bead-chain attached to the toy works nicely. All you need to do is to provide guidance and repeat the action over and over again. Don't forget to supply a reward for success!

Once the three basic tricks have been mastered, what your bird can learn is limited only by your imagination and patience. There is no end to the surprises a young cockatiel will provide for you.

If you purchase a healthy cockatiel (*above*) and make every effort to keep it healthy, by offering a well-balanced diet and by keeping the bird in a clean, spacious, draft-free environment, then you will get many years of enjoyment from your pet. Before you know it, your cockatiel will become an important member of the family and will come to regard your home as its own (*facing page*).

Talking

As you begin to think about teaching your cockatiel to talk, keep in mind that some birds are more adept at talking than others. There is a great deal of difference in the learning ability of each individual bird. This is one of the reasons for stressing the importance of getting to know your bird and its moods and working with the bird when it is most teachable. Regardless of the individuality of your bird, you can be assured that with perseverance just about any cockatiel, even an older one, can be taught to mimic at least a few words.

The actions taken in preparation for training are very important. No bird will be ready to talk unless it feels comfortable and relaxed in the company of its trainer. As you prepare to teach the first few words to your cockatiel, you must protect your bird from becoming frightened by other pets or noisy youngsters; you must especially guard the bird against sudden sounds and abrupt movements.

This is one reason why the location of the cage is so important. The bird should be placed where it is able to see what is going on, but the location must be safe enough and far enough away from the hustle and bustle of the household so that it will not become alarmed or distracted. Perhaps the most important ingredient of the training recipe is you. Give your bird attention and kindness so that it will come to love and trust you—and success is almost guaranteed. The sound of your voice and the attachment your pet is starting to develop for you are quite important.

The sex of the bird has no definite bearing on its ability to imitate. Cockatiels of both sexes have learned to talk. But you can expect that the younger the bird is, the more rapid will be its progress. The secrets of teaching a cockatiel to talk are *patience, perseverance,* and *constant repetition.* Aside from a few qualifiers, that's all there is to it.

One must always remember that a talking bird does not reason and does not understand the words it repeats. The bird only mimics the words it hears and repeats only by rote. If you choose to teach your bird words that are inappropriate for general use, you will have no one but yourself to blame when it embarrasses you. Talking birds seem to pick up swearing quite easily. This is because such expressions are usually spoken clearly and distinctly, often somewhat louder than the normal speech level.

Since the bird has become used to speech that is soothing and soft, when you begin to teach it to talk, chances for success will be enhanced if you use a louder voice than usual—remember that all birds belonging to the parrot family like noise and pay more attention to a loud voice than to a soft one. Up to this point you have attempted to gain your pet's confidence by using softly spoken words; now the only words spoken should be the ones you are trying to have the cockatiel learn. It's all right to continue to speak softly to the bird, but speak loudly, clearly, and distinctly during training sessions.

Some who have had a great deal of experience with cockatiels believe that talking lessons should be given while the bird is perched on the trainer's finger. Other experts feel that the practice distracts the attention of the bird and that teaching should be accomplished with the bird in the familiar and secure surroundings of its cage. You will have to decide which environment is the least distracting to your bird. There are trainers who feel the best way to gain the bird's attention is to conduct the training with the cage covered. This practice is not generally followed, although employing this method for the very first session of the day, as well as the last, is not without merit.

To actually teach the cockatiel to talk, the trainer should pick out just *one* word to start with. Begin with something simple, perhaps the bird's name or a single-syllable word, and repeat it several times. Say the word over and over again for about fifteen minutes, then end the lesson. Do not insert other words or phrases into the conversation; doing so will only serve to confuse your pet. Repeat the word each time you pass the bird's cage. Conduct training sessions several times a day, if possible. If not, at least two, one in the morning and one in the evening, will eventually do the trick.

Each time you repeat the word, use the same intonation; try not to change the way you repeat it. The first word you teach should be repeated slowly, with a pause between each repetition. Words that are strongly accented are preferred, at least in the beginning, as are higher pitched sounds.

In your eagerness to communicate with the bird, don't make the mistake of using "bird talk." If the bird gets the impression you are going to speak its language, it won't bother to learn yours.

Many cockatiels are inclined to whistle. This attempt at communication should not be encouraged, as many cockatiel owners have found that, however much they enjoyed the sound at first, with time it can be particularly annoying. Besides, the bird may be whistling instead of talking. Another cockatiel sound that may be mentioned is hissing. This is a normal response when a cockatiel is disturbed or frightened. As your cockatiel becomes accustomed to you, the hissing should disappear.

You will hear that some cockatiels have said their first word in a few weeks; don't be dismayed if it takes much longer for your bird to repeat its first word. Once it has mastered its first word, though, it will learn others more rapidly. But don't add a new word until your pet has fully mastered the first one. Constant repetition is the basis of successfully teaching a cockatiel to speak. If you are teaching a phrase, when the next word is added, *always* repeat the preceding word or words before the new one. If you continue in this way, your cockatiel will soon amaze you with the extent of its vocabulary. You will also find that your bird will pick up and repeat words that have not been deliberately taught to it; these words or phrases will be those frequently repeated in its presence.